CW00432926

More Praise For]

"Reading Kevin Ridgeway's first full-length collection Too Young To Know is like being on an adrenalized bi-polar thrill ride. These poems are urgent narratives taking place in trashy white neighborhoods populated with a parolee father shooting up during a matinee movie, bargain-bin-Barbie-look-alikes that fuel bouts of masturbation, hints of tender love, mental ward arts and crafts, a fat Jim Morrison, and his adored hippie-cool mother who dies too young. Their full tilt boogie rhythms are filled with singing syllables and slashing images that leave you stunned with their quirky beauty and relieved that the poet is hanging tough, struggling to make it through his days. Buy it. Now."

-Tony Gloeggler

"Suffering doesn't necessarily lend itself to art, but when it does you can get a heartrending, truly funny, razor sharp but gentle, first full-length collection like Kevin Ridgeway's *Too Young to Know*. Besides, a host of usual gifts, Ridgeway's got a hard-earned, very rare, acute sense of real life absurdity. Think R. Crumb, John Kennedy Toole, and yeah, Bukowksi. And his doll poems bring to mind work of Hans Bellmer. I only allude to these artists, because like them, he's a true original."

-Ted Jonathan

"Kevin Ridgeway is the real deal. Of course, Ridgeway has been on my radar for a long time because we're both bipolar, and few write about mental health as well as Kevin does. There's more to this collection. Much more. The heartbreaking first poem is a eulogy for his mother, and family ends up playing a big part in this book. Ridgeway takes us on a hell of a trip with Too Young to Know. All the way, he guides us through a range of emotions with a deft, artful touch. You want to read and own this book."

-Daniel Crocker

Too Young to Know

Poems by Kevin Ridgeway

STUBBORN MULE PRESS

DEVIL'S ELBOW, MO

Stubborn Mule Press

Devil's Elbow, MO

stubbornmulepress.com

Copyright ©Kevin Ridgeway, 2019

First Edition 1 3 5 7 9 10 8 6 4 2

ISBN: 978-1-950380-11-4

LCCN: 2019935865

Design, edits and layout: Jeanette Powers

Author photo: Elder Zamora

All rights reserved. No part of this publication may be reproduced or transmitted in any form or by any means, electronic or mechanical, including photocopying, recording or by info retrieval system, without prior written permission from the author.

Acknowledgments:

The American Journal of Poetry, Arroyo Seco Press, Bank-Heavy, Blink-Ink, Cadence Collective, The Cape Rock, Chaffey Review, Chiron Review, The Commonline Journal, Crisis Chronicles Press, Cultural Weekly, Drunk Monkeys, East Jasmine Review, Electric Windmill, Emerge Literary Journal, Gutter Eloquence Magazine, Home Planet News, Illya's Honey, Kleft Jaw, Lummox Press, Main Street Rag, The Mas Tequila Review, Misfit Magazine, Mojave River Review, Nerve Cowboy, Nixes Mate Review, The Orange Room Review, Plainsongs, Portraits in Poetry, Red River Review, Red Shift, Re)verb, RCC Muse, Rusty Truck, Samizdat, San Pedro River Review, Slipstream, Spillway, Suisun Valley Review, Thirteen Myna Birds, Trailer Park Quarterly, Unlikely Stories, Up the River, Verdad, Verse Virtual, Whiskey Fish Review and Yellow Chair Review.

CONTENTS

For My Mother,
Darci Lynn Ridgeway
(1954-2015)

I'm Not Ready to Write a Poem About My Mother's Death

but i can remember screaming
and collapsing
the phone and my brother's voice
shattering on the floor
after he told me what her brother
told him over the phone
and i still do not know
how to feel about
the love she abruptly
left behind with me
after all the years
we held onto
each other
for dear life.

Dead Relatives

All the Christmas Eve guests
are now buried or incinerated
corpses.

I need to write Santa for
a new family next year.

And he'll give me underwear
to humiliate me in front of
all the laughing ghosts.

Popeye

For Robert Altman (1925-2006)

the familiar whistle-rattling theme music
would play endlessly on our ancient television,
the lump-jawed visage and bulbous appendages
of my animated underdog hero and his
broken record chuckle, fighting bearded hulking
brutes in honor of his lank-legged brunette sweetheart
propelled by canned greens that helped him clean up
shop in a masterfully awkward dance that came to a
climax at the second of two reels
I worshipped this odd character, donned a secondhand
sailor suit, kept a plastic toy pipe tucked firmly in my
cherubic jowls and mumbled witticisms for the
kindergarten nerd girls that I fancied; I ate straight
out of aluminum cans and tried my hardest to flex
my arms until they swelled like balloons and chased
fools across schoolyards in the name of lunch pail
justice while they all laughed at my devotion to
this fantasy—
I grew too big for the sailor suit, switched to
cigarettes and grew enough hair and flab to
resemble the mean old mad-eyed heavies that
my quirky idol detested; I even switched to organic
vegetables, no more strength out of the kitchen
dry goods pantry...and I'm too deranged to join the navy

deep inside my sweet and salty exterior, beyond the
scars from the savage licks of adult life is that
strange boy in the sailor suit shadow boxing the
nightmares and evil goons away, squinting at the
bright lights of the old Technicolor cartoons that
are playing on the decaying television sets of
his mind.

Dented Grandpa

a photograph from
their 50th wedding
anniversary shows
the rose colored
indentation at the
center of his head
that they all say
he sustained at
ten years old when
a large mule kicked
him there inside the
family barn in Illinois
which revealed why
he had the ability to
cuss loudly in Thrifty
Drug without a care
and embarrass my
grandmother by
refusing to wait in the
car for the prescription
pills that she hoped
would cure all the
side effects from
a blow to the head
that made him so
goddamn stubborn.

The President of My Fan Club

I was waiting on a bench
at a suburban library for my
girlfriend to join me for an
afternoon reading magazines.
While old men disturbed the
peace with their walking farts,
a group of developmentally
disabled people and their aides
descended upon me and my
paperback of Anthony Burgess
dystopian literature. A diminutive
girl who let out earth shattering
howls and one word exclamations
sat right beside me and began to
slowly pet my long blonde hair,
murmuring *pretty* every few
seconds, as I calmly thanked her
and the aide asked me if I minded.
I politely said *no* as my admirer
lavished me with attention.
I whispered Warren Zevon lyrics
to her, and that crooked smile
grew wider with each deafening
wail as people dropped overdue
books through metal slots,
trying not to look

When Grandma Met Elvis

a photograph
sits on the
fireplace mantel
her proud smile
beneath her
perm standing
side by side
with Elvis
holding a
microphone
his mouth agape
frozen in time

she glanced
at it every
afternoon
and insisted
that The King
was a gentleman
and that they had
such a lovely time
together,
regardless of
the large sign
behind them
that read

Movie Land Wax Museum

What Grandpa Left Behind

the backyard was all
split shards of concrete
and twisted metal
surrounding a battered
swing set I sat upon
an old stove with ashes
from a ten-year old
fire and a locked wooden
shack stood decorated
with black widow
spider webs across
all of his old tools—
he was long dead,
and he left the
ruins of his
ancient toys
to no one.

1981

my dad spent the year
in prison, but my mother
still accepted his proposal.
they stand there in a
faded polaroid, the tattoos
on his arms blurred in
a mire of aqua green,
his shirt sleeves rolled up
with a cigarette sticking
out of his left cuff,
the numbers across his
chest easy to read
the year before I was
born, two years until
he got new inmate
numbers in 1983.

17th Street

she bakes the French bread
in the backroom
smoking half a cigarette
underneath the 3 am moonlight
the back door ajar
massaging her hair
underneath her employee cap
adjusting her upside down badge

8am rolls around in a stupor
and she announces this French bread
is on sale into a stale old PA microphone
with a genius for wordplay
snd a savvy for sales

3PM rolls along like the
morning didn't exist
snd she pulls onto 17th street
with a wedding cake in her trunk
up to the winding hills
of Anaheim,
searching for the stray balloons

6PM approaches, time to
start counting endless

receipts and quirky scribbling
on them to make the bank
for the dozens upon dozens
of goods sold that day

she comes home for me to
massage her neck, falling
asleep with a lit cigarette
In her mouth
I put it out.

Kool Aid Mustache

My playmates were dressed
like miniature bar flies
as we played hide and go seek
in the rubble of a collapsed cinder block wall
littered with broken chemistry sets
and shards of rotgut wine bottles
the blocks once help fortify this burned-out
property when they were a meth lab
but now the ruins were our playground
I hid beneath a stack of discarded egg cartons
my Velcro shoes sticking out
in a budding clown's cry for help
I was found in an instant and tagged *it*
by the girl with the runny nose
and the Kool Aid mustache
I counted to ten and spent an eternity
searching for these old pros
and gave up
retiring to the safety
behind the screen door
in the darkness of electric summer fans
dragging my soles across the carpet that
led to the console of television
and I fixed a stiff one
sitting in the serenity of my post-toddler
command center,
I sipped my sugared concoction and
grew a Kool Aid mustache of my own.

She Was the Man

I followed my brother and his
gang of friends around, often
excluded from their misadventures,
most notably when they pitched
a tent and camped out in our
mother's backyard in the
spooky wilderness of blue collar
suburbia. I hung out with my
mother in her red satin nightgown,
her hair in curlers to remain
beautiful for my father when he
got out on parole. The guys ripped
a huge hole in the tent and decided
on a night in front of the Atari
instead, playing Fight Night with
a phallic cherry joystick, my brother
motivated to pummel his pixelated,
slow moving opponents after his
friends teased him with a cassette
recording they found of him
beat-boxing and doing a falsetto
rendition of Stand by Me, which
I thought was the Holy Grail,
superior to the Whoopee Cushion
in its joy born out of all that is
off key and wrong about the

sound in the world, our former
blues singing prodigy of a Mom
smoking her Marlboro's and
teaching my brother's friends
who Big Mama Thornton was.
A Mom who was cooler than
her sons could ever dream to be.

Cheshire Cat

His role in the play came late in the game, and he was a
revelatory mystery in a flat cap and stripes, standing in the
shadows beneath a talking set piece painted to resemble the
Cheshire Cat, who he gave a beatnik voice to and from that
performance on he was a renegade who stole every show, no
longer uncomfortable exposing his bodily instrument and
the endless twists and turns of his emotional psyche as he
sharpened his craft into a revolutionary trajectory into the
wonderlands hidden in a cruel world he helps people escape
from, confront, laugh at and maintain a righteous hope for, a
cat who I followed down the rabbit hole where it was nearly
off with my head, the same head with eyes glued to the dim
spotlights at a brother who placed many of my wildest
dreams within reach like a supernatural cat in a hallucinatory
world full of revelations like him on that stage where he
found the dreams he had always been searching for and he
was the first in our DNA to rise above a fear to break free of
the silence which killed the rest of our family.

Breakfast in 1987

endless marathons of Gilligan's Island
starting in the wee small hours
of the weekday mornings
while we waited for the weekend
and Uncle Mike's red Toyota truck
sailing down Beach Boulevard
my brother and I lying
down in the truck bed
bouncing and crushing
our skulls along the way
to Bolsa Chica State Beach
the frown of lights at the
lonesome Jack in the Box
greeting us as we
prepared to body surf
while Mike would skid
atop his board along
the waves above our
heads, the fire pits
that dotted the sands
still smoldering from
the night before
the sun peaking out
through the maze of
clouds shaped like

Grandma's fried potatoes
with a half-cooked egg yoke
in the middle forming a
shabby masterpiece; I always
wanted to try to eat that sky
and break my teeth against it
blood dripping along the
grainy asphalt as steam
rose from the outdoor showers
to awaken the lazy gods

Dollar Store Barbie

I begged my mother for one,
and she relented
a knockoff called Missy
with her blonde hair
and tiny rubber clothes
that I took off in my toy room
to find not even a nipple
or a crack to form an ass
let alone a vagina
which was the whole point
I thought she was cute, though,
and I called her my girlfriend
until she got accidentally
decapitated by the vacuum
cleaner

I didn't see an actual vagina
until years later when a friend
opened up an old back issue of
Hustler Magazine
with its hardcore parade
of women and their in tact
parts spread out in full
color on dirty paper,
a parade of nasty wet dreams
come true, all of which
made me pine for Missy
and her eternal plastic
innocence

We'll See

those are the words
my mother told me
when I asked her
if I would grow up
to be president
of the united states

they were the same words
she spoke when I
asked her if it was
a good idea
to get married

the same phrase
she uttered
when I asked if
I was going to
earn a doctorate
in English literature

again, when I asked
if it was a good idea
to trade lithium
for Phenobarbital
tablets while balancing

myself naked on
the diving board
over our empty
swimming pool,
screaming at the
sun and wondering
if I might crack my
skull:

we'll see

Boogie Board Dick Rash

we rode the waves
at Bolsa Chica
and scratched at each
irritated scrotum on up
to our mushroom tips for
an oceanic salt water
marinated case of
boogie board dick rash,
and sand crept up our
asses while we ate
overpriced boardwalk
hot dogs and dreamed
of going home.

Creepy Dolls

there was no denying
her affection for
corrupted baby doll heads
factory reject Betsy Wetsies
and the plain Jane
strange girls that lined
our apartment,
trophies of the ongoing
freak tournaments that
she held like putty in the
palm of her ravaged mind
when we divorced
she won full custody
of our junkyard children
driving away with them
in baby car seats
headed for future
oblivion along the
highway paved with
scorched plasticity

Don't Get Your Hopes Up

five infamous, hand-me down
syllables of warning hidden
in the blinding, dirt cloud
exhalation of my Mother's
first after work cigarette
whenever my expectations
got a little too high that
helped prepare me for
all of life's inevitable
failures she could more
than guarantee from her
own bitter lifetime.

she absent-mindedly
disposed of her
cigarette in my
ice cold can of Pepsi,
and I choked on it
during negotiations
over how much of her
hard-earned spare
change I could feed into
the glowing, mechanized
slots of a limited selection
of outdated arcade games

responsible for so many
wasted childhoods at the
local neighborhood
liquor store, right beside
an overstocked shelf of
pornographic magazines
that would keep something
up when I got old enough
to feel hopeless.

School Bus Legend

I became an instant celebrity at the back
of that smoking yellow aluminum travesty
and it's potpourri of body odor fogging up
the windows when I ate a dried up remnant
of my own mucous to shock and awe.

I very quickly became infamous for my hidden
talent. At lunch time kids would whisper *It's
him* as I passed by with my corn dog covered
in wiggling peaches misplaced by the lunch
lady as she beamed at me and gave me extra
tater tots, having heard about my leap to the
top of the first grade social hierarchy.

my time in the spotlight was cut short when
another kid on the bus home belched out the
chorus of the song *Smooth Criminal* and I was
all washed up, my once popular show cancelled
and replaced with some hack who stole my act
when he bit off his own scab.

Laxatives

I thought I was clever
had found some candy
at four years old
in mother's bathroom
drawer

I ate the whole bar
and she caught me
a ring of chocolate
around my mouth
my stomach started
rumbling and a
parade of shit
flew out of my
little ass for hours

I was shaken,
had learned
an important
lesson--

I celebrated
by making
a sculpture
out of her
tampons

Wrestlemania

the garbage I watched on television
eating grandma's burnt-bacon sandwiches
cheering at strange men in superhero costumes
pummeling each other with folding chairs
and bad acting
has formed a huge part of who I am,
deep down in this strangeness.

'

Simon Bernstein

Was my best friend until his parents plucked him
out of elementary school in order to home school him.
He was replaced by a kid named Ruben Alvidrez,
an inferior stand-in who made strange duck sounds
and once slapped me in the face to my parent's delight.
Simon was no such droog. He was a fart smith,
happy to put on his best Curly Howard face
and nyuck it up like a fat jolly retard from hell.
Ruben was Dick Sargent to Simon's Dick York.
They both abandoned me in the end.

Two Dimensional Lovers

my mother had to look at every item on
sale at every department store we went
into and she always made these bargain
hunts ten times worse when she dragged
me into the forbidden aisles of the lingerie
department filled with women as they held
up their potential unmentionables that I ran
into, trying not to look at them, but that
changed with puberty when I even gawked
at the scantily clad headless mannequins
and, wearing only a skimpy black lace
negligee and gazing down lustfully at me
from her massive fading Montgomery Ward
poster advertisement was my sweetheart
that I secretly called Sharlena, her never
ending smile making out with me when I
saw the shell shocked faces of other sons,
frightened refugees smoked out of their
cavernous mall video arcade hideouts,
and the heartbreaking day came when they
replaced Sharlena with a homely woman
modeling a bra that was first introduced
at the 1939 World's Fair and I was unable
to track down my captive Sharlena before
wrecking balls shattered through that

confusing land of cup sizes, peek a boo
nighties and support hose that cried
pervert at me for peeping before I had
grown old, dirty and creepy enough to
get arrested for still hanging around
women's lingerie departments and when
security asks me what the hell I think I'm
doing, I'll tell them I'm waiting for
Sharlena.

Sleepover

the sleeping bags
were twisted together
and our PJ's were full
of sweat and urine
as we attempted to explain
to Jimmy's stepmother in
between spirited high five's
that we all had the greatest
experience of our lives
the night before, and no one,
including her, could ever take
those six wild over-sugared
hours in which we raised
all-in-onesy, headgear hell
away from us, Nintendo
tans and all.

The 1988 Sears Christmas Catalogue

it was epic: I wanted every toy in that
volume that weighed more than me, drooling
over sprawling train sets with routes through
holes in candy mountains; a James Bond
spy kit for kids with x ray glasses and
dynamite; a Lon Chaney Jr. as The Wolfman
doll that claimed to have real werewolf hair,
and other treasures I begged Santa Claus
for in a long chicken scratch letter written
in green crayon.

the big day came, and all I got from the
catalogue was a Stan Laurel ventriloquist
doll that I didn't ask for. it looked just like me,
and he and I entertained the adults for hours ,
who laughed and pinched my bare fat as I tried
to interact with my little smiling doppelganger.

the extensive lingerie section in the
catalogue came in handy a few years later,
and I had girls to yearn for and practice
impressing with my mastery of the
Stan Laurel dummy, his plastic smile
unmoving, not warning me ahead of
time that those girls would unwrap me
from my packaging and give me a try,
before they all tossed me aside.

Leftover Goulash

she had just quit drinking and smoking,
a greasy mountain of hamburger slowly
browning and beans simmering, her
secret ingredients borrowed from
Scandinavian and Irish roots while
we all sat in the living room watching
MC Hammer get 2 Legit to Quit in a
Taco Bell commercial on the widescreen,
his parachute pants saving him in a fall from
a skyscraper while he bit into an oversized
Taco Supreme

I asked her if I could have parachute pants
for Christmas, and she gave me that crinkle
eyed look and a raspy whisper of my name
that in tone alone admonished me enough
before hollering *soup's on* and all of us
piled around her table and ripped her
delicate layout to shreds, Hungarian inspired
sauces dripping off our chins that we washed
down with Pepsi Cola, the miniature dining
room television turned on and we watched
Vanilla Ice on an award show, hanging on to
every single one of his very few words

she stood at the kitchen counter without
saying a thing, brooding with indecision about
which recipe she should quietly clean her wounds
with and have plenty of leftovers for nuked lunches
she didn't have to serve while she dreamed of the
glory she cooked up in the past and it's drunken
mirage of perfection.

Skipping School

grandma's mind was fading
just as mine was growing
at seven-thirty in the morning
on most school days in the eighth
grade I would venture off
to the local greasy spoon
for breakfast, carrying my
paperbacks with me

only to return home at eight-thirty
in the morning, announcing that
the school day was over

in her senility she believed me,
and I would make nachos,
watch old silent movies,
listen to Al Jolson and
read old movie fan magazines
from the 1930s
the platinum blondes
of the ladies
blinding me of the
truth of my pitiable
little existence when
I was thirteen years old
and actively masturbating
my brains out

she would boil her coins,
talk to my dead
grandfather
play solitaire
and drink her own
perfume by mistake

we would share a ten o'clock
cup of coffee, her and I
after I had fed my bad report
card to the toilet, both of
us cheering on our own
insane victories

My Old Gym Shorts

the horrific memories
of eighth grade gym class
were finally laid to rest
when I donated my old
gym shorts to the local
thrift store

one day, while waiting
for a light to change,
I noticed an old woman
pushing a baby carriage
wearing a pair of
unmistakable navy
blue shorts with my
full name written on them
in permanent marker

they were my old gym shorts,
and I could not help
but scream
and heads turned
including the old woman's

if only she knew
all of the sweat
and blood

and tears
and nervous farts
that went into
those shorts

she'd
give them
up, too

Terminal Island

is grey and smells like tuna guts
the guards pad us down and stamp
our wrists in yellow mustard stink
VISITOR
he's in a wheelchair
never to walk again
a lie
he would walk out of those gates
several times and several chances
to get straight
and went on to outlive my mother
doing a life sentence
upstate
where it doesn't
smell like tuna guts
but it's silent
like all the answers
he may never hold.

Rico Suave

The tween ladies adored him,
and the teachers gave out extra
credit to him for being so handsome.
He was a pillar of the sixth grade
community, sweeping every awards
assembly and holding doors open
for the special needs kids. He was
the only guy in our class who had
a mustache, a sign of his advanced
maturity. He also sat next to me,
and he liked to whisper *you're nothing
but white trash* over and over again
into my ear before spitting directly
into my face. I made feeble attempts
to defend myself, but he always
blinded me with his palm and said
talk to the hand, the teacher diffusing
the situation by blaming it all on me.
He complained to her that I forgot
to wear deodorant, and the entire
class burst into a kind of mocking
laughter I never got used to, from
the time he sucker punched me in
the school cafeteria to the time he
ruined my favorite polo shirt during

a class pizza party after he smeared
pink cupcake icing bedazzled by
multicolored sprinkles against my
chest, and their laughing faces poked
voo doo doll holes that stung. Our
teacher yelled at me yet again; the
detention she gave me spelled out
my ongoing social condemnation in
blackboard chalk that was chipping
away slowly into pulverized dust.

Sawdust Memories

Uncle Mike opened the paint spackled
garage door as the overhead lights all flickered
on simultaneously; massive saw machines stood
caked in white dust in every corner of the shop,
and unfinished wood furniture scattered across
transparent tarps waited for him to grind them
from their orphanages into the homes of families
in the rich neighborhoods that dotted the hills
above the main drag of our southern California
bedroom community, the L.A. skyscrapers
in the distance as the sun bathed
the parking lot in an orange ethereal light
Mike gave me my first job that day,
a pint sized sidekick of four years on this earth
I swept the sawdust that rained from murdered wood
until we could see the concrete floor at long last
he pawed two dollars out of his pocket and paid
me my first wage, and I felt cheated for the first time
having hoped for a Lincoln five
I swept those floors every weekend,
yellow tornadoes swirling around me until I could
afford to take my grandmother and her paper skin
to the picture show, where we flew far away
from this dreary suburban dungeon of child labor,
scant wages and a legion of strangers' faces as they

wrote in their checkbooks and my uncle loaded their
trucks with brand new dressers and coffee tables
my cherubic face hidden in anonymity behind
a disposable surgical mask, envisioning
myself on celluloid basking in the lush front lawns of
castles made of gold and not wood
I swept those floors and I would pretend
the broom was Ginger Rogers
and I was a deranged Fred Astaire
I danced furiously as the saw screamed
daggers into my ears, my fingers bleeding
from the splinters that danced all around me
my Uncle Mike, the woodworking tycoon
smiled at me from behind massive
plastic goggles, his eyes saucers as he
carved out people's cookie cutter dreams.

Size Husky

It made my ears tingle and I held back
nervous vomit whenever my mother said
those words too loudly in the boy's clothing
aisle of JC Penney, the stench of death in
the air when she held up wide pairs of junior
denim pants like maps for wars that I could
not win, while other kids and their mothers
laughed and mocked me in Spanish.

My older brother got slapped once after
calling her a bitch for saying those words
in reference to his own expanding waist line,
so I knew I couldn't fight dirty and had to
remain patient with her as she ruined my
social life before the school year even began,
calling out my name and asking me what
size underwear I wore as I peeked out of
flimsy dressing room curtains that did little
to hide my shame, and I shuddered while
trying to remember all the details for the
day when I would be able to afford therapy,
a licensed professional staring off into space
and daydreaming while I blubbered into a
Kleenex linked to my nose by one long
hair of angst-ridden snot.

Twenty Seconds to Stink Bomb Detonation

we could see
our teacher's
scrotum hang-
ing from his
shorts on the
Ferris wheel
at the same
carnival I barfed
cotton candy
& cheese bagel
dog into my lap
after riding
the Mexican
teacups that
had a family
of possums
living under-
neath them who
caused a serious
and prolonged
outbreak of
monster lice
at school that our
parents blamed
on the flying
cockroach
problem we
had at home.

Prom in the Year 1999

the Polaroid her father
took shows me in an ill fitting
tuxedo, my Aqua Net polluted
accidental white boy
Little Richard hair
towering above an acne ridden
face that was too small for its
forced smile
standing arm in arm
with a beauty in bridal white
her vanilla ice cream hair coupled with
a smile whose wattage was bright
enough for reciprocating camera flashes
and the pages of Seventeen.

the dance floor
was over a shark tank at the
Long Beach Aquarium; I stepped
on her foot a half a dozen times
peering at the hammerheads
wiggling their fins to *Pretty*
Fly For a White Guy. we had
that opportune moment alone
in the darkness of the captive
sea, but I hesitated for too long
and I sat in my tuxedo at home

by eleven, watching the
latest breaking news car chase
and smelling my breath in my
hand for clues to the mystery
behind the rental fees of an
overpriced belly flop

she didn't speak to me until
I got up enough nerve to ask her to
sign my yearbook on the last
day of school, and she
squinted through her inscription.
she handed my annual back
and whispered *good bye* with
a wide step away from me and
down the hall, her short dress
pitying me as they both moved on
and everyone crowed a unified
hallelujah praising the gods of
summer

the Polaroid blushes with
apologies regarding its subjects
when discovered hiding in
scrapbooks with pleas to my mother
to skip over it as she pours evidence into
the laps of new girlfriends who try
to rescue me from these blooper
reels and the sense memories of

that rotting corsage that fell from
my date's wrist that I couldn't find
in the darkness of an audience
of bored jellyfish staring back at us,
wiggling upward to the vibrations of Prince
grooving from a popular 1982 song, but,
unlike him, we were too afraid to party
like it was 1999.

My Mother's 1970 Yearbook

I would always pull it off of the
bookshelf and get lost in its
floods of mini skirts in mostly
black and white with the occasional
color shots that made them all look
like they were on an old episode
of Love American Style:
beautiful young women in curled hair
teasing my loins thirty years in advance.

they made me want to jump into the pages of
their yellow spine worn volume of other
hazy memories and disrupt the
space time continuum by
coming face to mirrored face with my
mother's two foot high beehive and
scalp tickets for the Flying Burrito Brothers
to girls who keep calling me *man* in
the dying restroom smoke
of drowned cigarettes in flushing toilets
before they ask me if I have any whites
or reds and its these kinds of things
that help me to stop daydreaming and
deal with the weirdness of my own time,
and hopefully meet a girl along the way
who likes miniskirts.

Poem I Might Have Written But Have Since Lost

I drank the two rolling rocks
my father left behind when
he violated his parole
blasting Fiona Apple
and discovering
Frank Zappa and
the Mothers of
Invention. fresh
out of the psych ward
after an emotional
breakdown and
suicide attempt.
a new high school
graduate whose
friends now treated
him like an unbalanced
weirdo. But not Ruby,
our class Salutatorian
on her way to study
at Yale. We hung out,
she introduced me
to her beloved Morrisey
and I shared my folder
of poems and plays
i hid from everyone.
then our group of
friends split up
for college,

on my way
to drunken
oblivion, but
I remember
Ruby and her
family's welcome
to me into their
home at
a time when
I'd never felt
more ignored.
unpopular
and prepared
to run off into
an unexpected
world in my
life and I'd
thank her
for teaching
me not to
be afraid to
be different
just not so
sad for warm
hearts like
her to worry
over while
they save
the world
and I brood
over it.

Garage King

my grandfather converted
it into a pool hall in the 1960s
and it's signature yellow shag
carpeting survived into the new
millennium. I returned to stay
temporarily but have lingered
a year or two longer than we
expected, T-Bone Walker's
bent strings howling out of
a stereo speaker while I pace
around the ancient billiards
table in my underwear, reading
a tabloid from 1973 that was
recently found in the attic, it's
pages crinkling into pieces of
nostalgic dust that I inhale while
it's ghosts pray for the moment
I put on my pants and never return,
leaving them to their after lives in
a museum of the past I don't
need to guard anymore.

Kamikaze Summer

early that last June of school,
I received dozens of get well
soon letters from classmates
in response to a week earlier
when I swallowed a bottle of
sleeping pills that landed me
in an adolescent psychiatric
ward, flowers and great big
stuffed animals waiting at
the front hospital desk.
I cannot remember much
about that day other than
all of the revisions my suicide
letter went through, and I nearly
lost my nerve with Brian Wilson
singing on top of a teenaged
symphony to God that made me
dwell too much on small tragedies,
and my brother flew out from
New York City not knowing
what to say while my teachers
all felt sorry for me enough
to pass me without completing
my final exams and rumors
that I was disfigured in my
feeble attempt at death were

quashed when I marched with
a class of over four hundred
students at our commencement,
still breathing but just another
lonely name they announced that
hot afternoon that echoed off
the bleachers of their football
stadium before it rocketed
beyond the clouds to the outer
limits of uncertainty.

Her Dead Husband's Ashes

She had told me about them,
where she stored them, and
I was perfectly fine with having
him around. She had been gone
for several days before I finally
opened the drawer and pulled
out the cardboard box that I
opened and there he was, a
pile of gray sand I had heard
so much about in her colorful
stories that I got nervous as
I said hello and introduced
myself. I was lonely, and he
completely understood. He
asked me for something to
drink so I got us some beers.
We laughed and talked until
sunrise. I got emotional about
her and he cheered me up by
letting me sort through him in
search of his remaining teeth.
All was going well with us
bachelors until the day the
Neptune Society came and
took him away to be scattered
like all the other people I get
too close to.

Advertisement for Myself

I open my eyes
and they are all
staring up at me
on my billboard
in designer
underwear
and they
have twisted
thoughts
about my
love handles
until I am
forgotten
about
when
they turn
into the
next aisle
where
they
browse
men's
socks
and
swimwear

while
I wonder
when I will
wake up
from this
nightmare
all alone
and in my
underwear.

ZaSu Pitts

didn't say a word in a publicity shot
draped in an unbuttoned
leopard print coat just enough
to expose where her mid thigh
met the lace hem of a slip
the color of two-reeler
pre-Hayes code
black and white indiscretion,
frozen in a colorless time
long before I was born to
be young, dumb and full
of unenlightened cum
and slowly daydreaming
myself into a great depression
of my own while she glared at me
from 1933 in the back row
of eighth grade social studies
in 1996 before I folded her up
and stuck her in my front pocket
until the next time I needed
a little hope as she rolled her eyes
at me from the darkness.

Buster Keaton Is Silent Forever

he's buried near Marty Feldman
not far from Stanley Laurel
a stone's throw from Scatman Crothers
and Jeff Porcaro
not to mention Bette Davis
who did it the hard way
but people pass by this cemetery
on their way to work making
more dreams for us to distract
ourselves from real life fears
such as death and the immortality
of even movie stars.

Ashland

a passenger side nap
ended with a glance up
at infinite: the Who
chanting they can see
for Miles and Miles
all the way up
redwood giants
whose tops we couldn't see
in the darkness of the road.
a Bakersfield car wash
Funk Classics, Volume Two
cassette tape brings it all
to a fever pitch when we pass
over Oregon state lines and
pull into Ashland; a hippie
chick with twin braids and legs
as long and beautiful as said
redwoods sang along to the
stereo speakers on a chorus
whose only word was *fun*
as she flashed a smile my way,
her sapphire eyes teasing me
with a wink at possibility,
and I suggested to my driver
that we stop there for the
night and leave our mark.

Let's All Go Out to the Lobby and Have Ourselves Some Smack

Dad kept leaving the movie
turns out he was shooting up
he nodded off and i thought he was bored
but in reality he was chasing a high since
he was the same age as i was, fourteen years old
when he began stealing and committing robberies
to support his escalating habit
i dressed like a combination between dennis the menace
and Steve Urkel
was a member of the Marx Brothers Fan Club
hung out with my 87 year old grandmother
more than most other people
and had not even kissed a girl,
let alone had the courage to talk to one.
but my Dad's life became a movie
at fourteen years old when i still daydreamed
of when life was going to finally start really happening
Dad was bored with the Woody Allen movie
he preferred Hell's Angels and gritty stories
about dope fiends or gangsters
or movies laden with dick jokes
so he shot up in the cinema restroom
and his face rested on top of a large tub
of popcorn and yelled *fuck* at the top

of his lungs when my mother nudged
him in the ribs to snap him out of it
and he complained that she was
messing with his high but for me he was
ruining what was really one of
Woody Allen's lesser efforts
at the time and I daydreamed that
my life would be a better movie than
it and my father's movies ever were.

Lost Music

growing up,
we had begged Mom for a piano
and our desire to break into music
was never honored.

but when we
moved out of the house,
Mom bought a fucking piano.

when she died, my brother
and I had to move the piano
out the front door of the house
we grew up in and were selling
along with the piano that crushed
our feet when we had to rest,
a modern day Laurel and Hardy—

in a struggle with a latter day
music box neither one of us
conquered with our boogie-less
fingers, and she sang
in our memories from
her vibrato urn.

Cosmic Space Fuck

she was seated by herself
in the front pulpit at one of
the dozens of chapels
at Rose Hills Memorial Park,
curious about the hoards
of Latino people as they
all drove in when she
realized she was at the
wrong funeral. The
grieving family moved
their parked cars out
from blocking hers
so she could be late
to the right funeral,
three weeks before
her own funeral was
held in that very same
chapel, alone yet again,
and far too early for
us all.

Parental Guidance Relinquished

my father
makes his
life sentence
go by faster
when he helps
sew the
uniforms
worn by
officers
in the line
of duty
the same
uniforms
they were
probably
wearing
when they
dropped me
off at a
special home
for orphaned
man child
survivors
of recently
deceased
mothers

who got
paroled
for good
behavior
from this
prison
where
we're
all doing
time.

Medication Time

We stood in a crooked line
that extended from the nurse's
station to the activities room,
dressed in our pajamas at three
on a Tuesday afternoon. We
peeled and scratched the Elmer's
glue skins from our hands in the
wake of arts & crafts group, where
I declined to create a self portrait
out of macaroni, instead laboring
over an elaborate beaded bracelet
I was going to give to the pretty
Armenian girl who overdosed on
New Year's Eve, having failed to
die like the rest of us had all
wanted to.

Nerves tickled my pumped stomach
when she kissed me on the cheek,
her packed bags in hand after she
scrawled her cell phone number on
the front of my Xeroxed Relapse
Prevention handout. I never saw her
again, but I was on top of the imaginary
world at the front of that line with that

bracelet hidden in my sweaty palm and
my mouth opened wide so that the
Filipino nurse could be sure I swallowed
my lithium, daydreaming about that
crazy girl mixed up with crazy me, both
of us far away from that ward of catatonic
lunch room Pictionary teammates in a
place where we would have more than
just the will to live.

My Drug Dealer's Girlfriend

several days after he beat
the marijuana smoke out
of me, I looked into her
bruised eyes over a grilled
cheese we split at Clifton's
downtown and agreed to
let her borrow money for
a Greyhound ticket.

we had been flirtatious
behind his back. she
revealed her bra to me in
paparazzi flashes when she
got drunk, and I showed her
my man tits and she helped
me try the bra on, which made
him wonder what we were
both laughing at.

weeks later, I received a
postcard she had filled out
in sloppy cursive from her
grandmother's house in
Lincoln, Nebraska. she
said she'd miss me and

asked for the name of a
Neil Young album I always
played for her, having left a
kiss made of crimson lipstick
in the margin underneath
my misspelled name.

I stayed behind in that drug
den the three of us inhabited:
just me and Neil wailing from
the grooves of that old vinyl
record, trapped there with our
lonely boy choir of a heartbreaking
song on parallel roads bound for
the same no where.

Crayons for Dessert

John commands everyone's
attention when he sings a
Smokey Robinson tune,
a long strand of drool hanging
from his outstretched, quivering
bottom lip that our mental health
counselor wipes off with the
torn first page of a brochure
on sexually transmitted diseases,
just as a dazed Haitian man
who brought a Boys II Men
album to our post-lunchtime
creative expressions group
forms a gun with his hand
and pretends to shoot himself,
which ignites a giggle fit in
the schizophrenic waiting room
bingo champion next to me
that sounds like a hundred
Pillsbury Doughboys trapped
inside of a blender. The
hypnotic leather jowls
of an old, washed up
beauty queen graze
the cardboard ruins

of a cup of noodle soup
box that she vandalizes
with her chicken scratch
notes of our biweekly
meetings in a crayon
the color of an artificial
Velveeta sunrise that
she slowly begins to
munch on, our counselor
oblivious as she whispers
into the electric razor
buzz shock of her newest
cell phone, aggravating
the side effects of our
medications, our mouths
opened wide so they
could be sure we didn't
cheek our pills.

I'm Going to Die Someday

and they'll use the insurance money
to buy a cheap plot of earth
next to the bulldozers
and the exhaust of the freeways

the preacher who didn't know me
will speak of Jesus Christ
and everyone will roll their eyes
because my church was rock n roll

my cheap pine coffin will be full of
splinters that cut my pall bearers'
fingers as they drop it clumsily
onto the elevator for worms

if they can afford a headstone,
it will be full of bullshit and lies
that say nothing about who I was
and the lawnmowers will ride
over it every week until it sinks
into the ground beneath rotten leaves

the world will breathe its stench
and its glorious beauty while
my skeleton withers in its

cheap Sears bought suit
tragedies will come that
I'll never see or know

it's better for me to live now
than agonize over the pain
of going back into the mystery
I came from, to dance to the
music and make love and
be a happy idiot screaming
over a billion lights that
will dim away like the end
of the psychic chants of
a spinning rock n roll
record full of dead voices
drifting into silence as the
needle on the cosmic player
comes to a halt.

Fat Jim Morrison

that's what he calls me when he ambles
out onto the porch, my cigarette in one
hand, my beard in the other with an entire
galaxy of suicidal flowers hanging from
my shoulders. I growl from a Doors
song, I've been down so goddamn long,
five years since I was the perfect age to
die bloated and full of heroin and absinthe
in a Parisian bathtub, my fans and admirers
throwing dirty graveside celebrations that
leave them more wasted than my short
life, but I have instead lingered beyond
such a fantasy with the reality of growing
too old to be a rock star, exhausted by
a career based on amateur theatrics
whose self-destructive choreography
has left the soundtrack to my life at near
bottom of the pop charts. My new front
yard companion slaps my large gut, takes
a sip of his root beer and proceeds to tell
me a long story about how he got so high,
he woke up old with his entire life behind
him in an inglorious fog, all alone with
no memories to wash away the pain of
unwanted survival.

Uh Oh, Gotta Go

Read the poolside sign at my grandparents' house,
a dated 1960s era cartoon kid with an ashamed
expression on his face and the request:

please, not in the pool.

I took a big shit in that pool once, and the kid
on that sign felt better about himself for a change,
and the sign disappeared with the years.

How to Win Friends and Influence People

I was too hip, slick and cool for the kids in the school musical:
ad libbing lines and having an overall bad attitude.
That's when the lead actress compared my poolside physique
to a holocaust victim and everyone busted up laughing.
I ran into the house where I hunted down my sweater and
my pressed chinos when the lead actresses' mother entered
the room, screamed as I draped my sweater over my hardon
as it peaked out of my boxers, and laughed when I began to
sing Nice Work If You Can Get It, which won her over and
saved my ass for another night in the hell of Los Angeles.

Playing Along to the Weird Music

he watched races and old science shows in the dark
of his living room, attired in swim trunks and a big
and tall plaid shirt still crinkling from its flat plastic
wrapping, every single window shade pulled down,
hiding from the sun and everyone else since my
grandmother dragged her luggage out the front door
decades earlier.

he loved jazz and bebop; it would drool from
a little fuzzy radio that he would adjust until he vaporized
an orchestra of static imposters trying to
jam behind Chet Baker. he did not allow me to fiddle with
the strange assortment of old engine parts that covered
his living room carpet, but he always let me play with
the distracting fleet of model cars and airplanes so
that he could set to work on building mini speed demons
for Sunday morning desert races, the only time he ever
bothered to wear pants.

one afternoon, Labyrinth starring David Bowie came on;
I sat on his lap and we watched Bowie steal infants and
croon space grooves with freakish cousins of the Muppets.
I could feel his gut tense and move up and down with laughter
and his heart sounded like a Gene Krupa drum beat that told
me he was not haunted by that same old lifetime of

disappointment but that he was as fresh and wide eyed as that same silly depression-era kid high on model airplane glue and still passionately daydreaming his way out of the labyrinths he had built around himself.

Have Mercy

that's what the old man kept yelling from a gurney
beside mine, both of us strapped down by our hands,
our feet, and our torsos. the nurses all cracked jokes
at his expense in between telling him to shut the fuck
up. he asked me to free him from his restraints, and
the crotch in his jeans interrupted my helpless reply
when it grew moist from an angry, desperate piss.
several hours and no Valium later, four EMTs carted
us both over to the twin doors of separate rigs for
our dusk freeway journeys to facilities where they
would free me from bondage, and could hear the
jingle-jangle of the metaphysical chains he enslaved
himself in for a doomsday not even Houdini could
escape from, just as I could taste personal quicksand
for the very first time, never to drown in my own
sorrows ever again.

Manhattan School of Confidence

I was 17 years old and barely a
hundred pounds soaking in my
own cum, pacing up and down
5th Avenue, trying to get up the
courage to ask for a job application
from The Gap

a beautiful woman among the throngs
removed her dress and began to
march naked, cutting through the
thick crowd on the sidewalk like
a rapier, everyone moving aside
with complete astonishment while
her bare breasts and shaved
vagina headed straight for me

I didn't know what to do
until she was came to a stop,
her nipples making eye
contact with me. she looked
down from her heels and
simply said,

get the fuck out of the
way!

I moved aside, never
to know why that had to
be my first time with
a beautiful, naked woman
and I looked on while her
smooth and confident ass
was photographed by tourists
and I went home jobless,
confident The Gap would
have stripped me bare only
to find my teenage lack of
everything before handing
my application back and
telling me to get the fuck
out of the way.

Nepotistic Scourge

i wanted to start my own franchise
get married to my college sweetheart
have kids
and stand out from the shadows
of a family who splintered
into opposing teams

i fumbled beyond the altar
drank scotch to impotency
and took up smoking
on my wedding day

i sit here, divorced

sixty days off drugs
and i wonder what
my dead mother is up to
and if i should write
my father a letter
while he ages in prison

while i ponder another
bump in the lonesome road
and break every link of
these chains

and pump the gas
on this lagging wagon
toward a destiny
behind the fog of
this life to a corner
of time's sandbox
where I belong

The Original Unsung Hometown Zero

I daydreamed in the grooves of vinyl LPs scooped up for
discounts in the rare expertise of Lovell's Record Store
on Greenleaf Avenue and hid in the claustrophobic stacks
of the Little Old Book Shop, terrified during auditions for
plays at the community theatre my brother, Richard Nixon
and I all performed in over the decades. Girls I had
crushes on saw me in my underwear behind that stage
during quick-change pants-drops in between scenes
onstage where they gave me my first kisses. I spent
so much of my time up in my head that I forgot to
experience Whittier much beyond my role as one of its
fallen stars, a drunk in the pews of Saint Matthias Church
listening to musicians eulogize the husband of my first
AA sponsor the week after my great grandmother died
and my father was sentenced to life in prison on the
front page of the Whittier Daily News. I whisper Happy
Mother's Day to him as a reminder of his wife's death
from inside those St. Matthias pews as I croon a
Sympathy for the Devil feared by dead poet John
Greenleaf Whittier who came from Haverhill,
Massachusetts where my college best friend grew up
and where we wrote bad poetry that had nothing to do
with two places where I never belonged, wasted
and in search of the eternal poet who writes verse that's
beyond all human comprehension, the one that saves me
in my newfound life as a rolling stone on my way to
finding myself, whoever that is but he's not in Whittier
or Haverhill. My mind is my hometown.

Death Stunt

one morning
while in a crystal
methamphetamine
twist
eyes bugged out
and pants barely staying up
I stood paranoid guard while
my psychiatrist and drug counselor
confronted me for being high
I stood up in melodrama footlights
to produce a small urn of my mother's ashes
that stunned them both
and I escaped up Long Beach Blvd.
through the streets of Ice Cube's Compton
with her ashes as my only
protection--
not from anyone else
but myself.

Kevin Ridgeway was raised in Whittier, CA. He has lived in New York City, Vermont, Massachusetts and Maine. He attended Goddard College but abandoned his studies for a failed early marriage, followed by several lost years suffering from untreated bipolar disorder during which time he embarked on a drunken public library and used book store self education with silent movies playing on his t.v. set and old school rock n roll grooving from his turntable. He began contributing to the small, independent and underground presses in 2010, and has remained prolific ever since. He is the author of nine chapbooks of poetry. A two-time Pushcart Prize and two-time Best of the Net nominee, he lives and writes in Long Beach, CA.

Printed in July 2019
by Rotomail Italia S.p.A., Vignate (MI) - Italy